SPACE SCIENCE

MERCURY

BY NATHAN SOMMER

BELLWETHER MEDIA · MINNEAPOLIS, MN

TM

Are you ready to take it to the extreme? Torque books thrust you into the action-packed world of sports, vehicles, mystery, and adventure. These books may include dirt, smoke, fire, and chilling tales. **WARNING**: read at your own risk.

This edition first published in 2019 by Bellwether Media, Inc.

Library of Congress Cataloging-in-Publication Data

Names: Sommer, Nathan, author.
Title: Mercury / by Nathan Sommer.
Description: Minneapolis, MN : Bellwether Media, Inc., [2019] | Series:
   Torque. Space Science | Audience: Ages 7-12. | Audience: Grades 3 to 7. |
   Includes bibliographical references and index.
Identifiers: LCCN 2018039177 (print) | LCCN 2018040669 (ebook) | ISBN
   9781681036922 (ebook) | ISBN 9781626179745 (hardcover : alk. paper)
Subjects: LCSH: Mercury (Planet)–Juvenile literature.
Classification: LCC QB611 (ebook) | LCC QB611 .S61975 2019 (print) | DDC
   523.41–dc23
LC record available at https://lccn.loc.gov/2018039177

Editor: Kate Moening   Designer: Andrea Schneider

Printed in the United States of America, North Mankato, MN.

TABLE OF CONTENTS

AN ICY DISCOVERY

It is October 2014. The *Messenger* spacecraft returns the first photos of Mercury's north pole to NASA. It is the only spacecraft to ever reach this area safely.

   Messenger's photos show huge ice chunks in Mercury's northern craters. How did the ice form on this tiny burning planet? Much of Mercury is still a mystery!

ILLUSTRATION OF *MESSENGER* AT MERCURY

WHAT IS MERCURY?

Mercury is the solar system's smallest, innermost planet. It is 3,032 miles (4,880 kilometers) across. This is only a little wider than the United States!

Mercury's dusty, cratered surface looks like Earth's Moon. But it is much bigger and hotter. Mercury's equator reaches 800 degrees Fahrenheit (427 degrees Celsius)!

FUN FACT

FROZEN GROUND

Mercury's poles and the far side from the Sun get very cold. They can reach -290 degrees Fahrenheit (-179 degrees Celsius)!

HOW FAR AWAY IS MERCURY?

EARTH TO MERCURY = 58,000,000 MILES (93,000,000 KILOMETERS)

MERCURY TO SUN = 35,000,000 MILES (56,000,000 KILOMETERS)

Mercury has a very weak atmosphere. Most of its gases are burned off by the Sun's heat. This gives Mercury its very hot and very cold temperatures.

Mercury also has a magnetic field. Earth and Mercury are the only rocky planets that have one. Both planets have an iron core that controls the field.

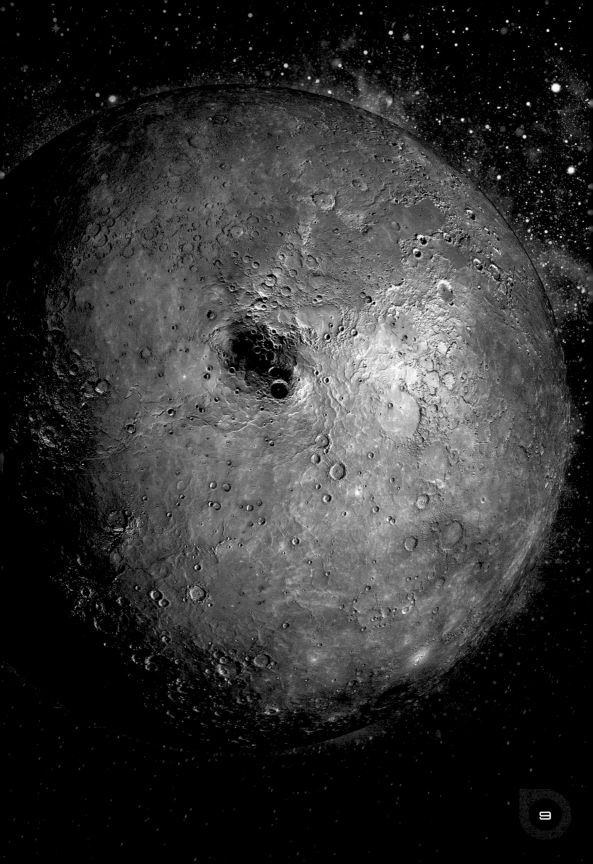

HOW DID MERCURY FORM?

Mercury formed with the other planets 4.6 billion years ago. It may once have been much bigger. Scientists think heat from the Sun wore down its surface. This may be why its thick, partly liquid core is over half of the planet's mass.

Mercury is slowly getting smaller. Its liquid iron core is cooling. The iron hardens as it cools. This causes the surface above to cave in. It has already sunk 4.4 miles (7 kilometers)!

CORE SIZE OF MERCURY VS. EARTH

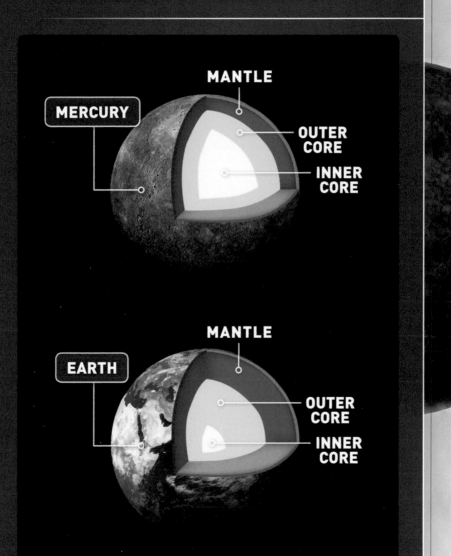

MERCURY

MANTLE

OUTER CORE

INNER CORE

EARTH

MANTLE

OUTER CORE

INNER CORE

ASTEROID

Powerful volcanoes helped shape
Mercury's surface about 3.5 billion years ago.
The surface is also shaped by asteroids.
With little atmosphere to burn them up, these
objects break apart and hit the planet often.
Many wide craters dot the landscape.

As Mercury's surface sinks, new cliffs
and valleys form. The largest of these
valleys is 2 miles (3.2 kilometers) deep!

CALORIS BASIN

FUN FACT

SUPER-SIZED CRATER

The Caloris basin is Mercury's largest crater.
It is 960 miles (1,545 kilometers) across.
This makes it larger than Texas!

WHERE IS MERCURY FOUND?

Mercury sits between the Sun and Venus. The planet orbits the Sun once every 88 days. It has the shortest years of any planet in the solar system! A day on Mercury lasts 58 Earth days.

Sometimes, Mercury crosses paths with Earth's orbit. When this happens, it appears as a black dot in front of the Sun.

FUN FACT

THE FASTEST PLANET
The ancient Romans noticed Mercury's short years. They named the planet after their speedy messenger god.

SUN

MERCURY

VENUS

FUN FACT

A HISTORIC FLYBY

NASA's *Mariner 10* was the first spacecraft to fly by Mercury. It passed Mercury in 1974. *Mariner 10* discovered the planet's magnetic field and weak atmosphere.

Mercury's location in space makes it hard to study. It rises and sets with the Sun, so it often disappears at night. Earth's thick atmosphere also makes it hard to see.

Mercury is also very hard to reach with spacecraft. Astronomers must create spacecraft that do not wear down in the heat.

WHY DO WE STUDY MERCURY?

When *Messenger* began orbiting Mercury in 2011, scientists began to learn more about Mercury. The spacecraft measured Mercury's core. It also discovered that the planet is getting smaller.

Mercury itself cannot support life. But its surface is covered with organics that make life on other planets. Scientists want to find out how they got there. This will help them understand how matter travels through space.

MESSENGER

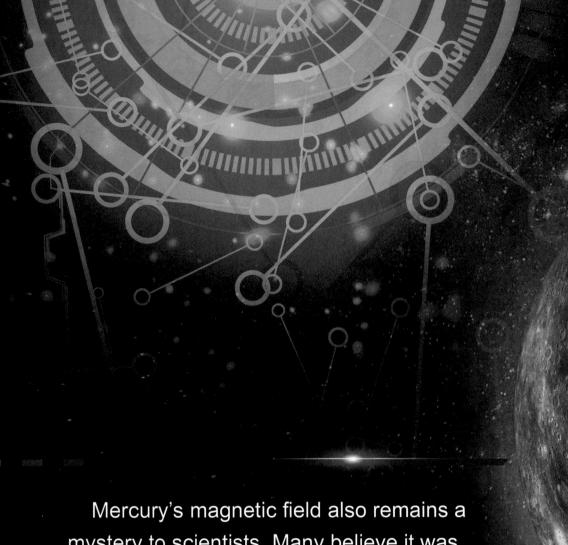

Mercury's magnetic field also remains a mystery to scientists. Many believe it was once much stronger but weakened over time. Finding out why it weakened will help them understand how planets like Earth age.

Mercury was once thought to be an empty desert. But this burning hot planet offers more than meets the eye!

GLOSSARY

asteroids–small rocky objects that orbit the Sun

astronomers–people who study space

atmosphere–the gases that surround Mercury and other planets

core–the innermost part of Mercury

craters–deep holes in the surface of an object

equator–an imaginary circle around a star or planet that is equal distance from each pole

magnetic field–an area around an object where a magnetic pull exists

mass–a measurement of how much matter an object is made up of

matter–the material something is made of

NASA–National Aeronautics and Space Administration; NASA is a U.S. government agency responsible for space travel and exploration.

orbits–moves around something in a fixed path

organics–materials that make up living things

pole–one end of a planet or star; every planet or star has two poles.

volcanoes–vents that let out hot rocks and steam

TO LEARN MORE

AT THE LIBRARY

Berne, Emma Carlson. *The Secrets of Mercury*. North Mankato, Minn.: Capstone Press, 2016.

Beth, Georgia. *Discover Mercury*. Minneapolis, Minn.: Lerner Publications, 2019.

Rathburn, Betsy. *The Sun*. Minneapolis, Minn.: Bellwether Media, 2018.

ON THE WEB

FACTSURFER

Factsurfer.com gives you a safe, fun way to find more information.

1. Go to www.factsurfer.com.

2. Enter "Mercury" into the search box.

3. Click the "Surf" button and select your book cover to see a list of related web sites.

 INDEX

The images in this book are reproduced through the courtesy of: Aphelleon, front cover, p. 2;
NASA /JHU/APL/ Wikipedia, pp. 4-5; NASA/Johns Hopkins University Applied Physics Laboratory/
Carnegie Institution of Washington/ NASA Images, pp. 6-7 (Mercury), 18-19 (Messenger), 19 (Mercury);
Vadim Sadovski, pp. 7 (Venus), 12-13 (asteroids); Iuliia Bycheva/ Alamy, pp. 8-9 (Mercury); xtock, p. 9
(Earth); NASA/JPL/Caltech/ NASA Images, pp. 10-11; Vadim Sadovski, pp. 12-13 (asteroids); Dotted
Yeti, p. 13 (Mercury); Vitaly Sosnovskiy, pp. 14-15 (Sun), 17 (Sun); tuntekron petsajun, p. 15 (planets);
Jurik Peter, pp. 16-17; NASA Images, pp. 20-21.